BITCOIN

HOW BITCOIN IS RESHAPING THE WORLD OF FINANCE

By K. Connors

© Copyright 2018 By K. Connors - All Rights Reserved.

Copyright © 2018 *Blockchain.* All rights reserved. No part of this publication may be reproduced, distributed, or transmitted in any form or by any means, including photocopying, recording, or other electronic or mechanical methods, without the prior written permission of the publisher, except in the case of brief quotations embodied in critical reviews and certain other noncommercial uses permitted by copyright law. This also includes conveying via e-mail without permission in writing from the publisher. All information within this book is of relevant content and written solely for motivation and direction. No financial guarantees. All information is considered valid and factual to the writer's knowledge. The author is not associated or affiliated with any company or brand mentioned in the book, therefore does not purposefully advertise nor receives payment for doing so.

Table of Contents

INTRODUCTION 4

CHAPTER 1 7

APPLICATIONS OF BLOCKCHAIN 7

CHAPTER 2 10

BLOCKCHAIN TECHNOLOGY 10

CHAPTER 3 15

THE WORKING OF BLOCKCHAIN 15

CHAPTER 4 20

USERS OF BLOCKCHAIN 20

CHAPTER 5 23

WHAT IS BITCOIN? 23

CHAPTER 6 28

CHARACTERISTICS OF BITCOIN 28

CONCLUSION 30

INTRODUCTION

If you've attempted to dive into this mysterious thing called blockchain, you'd be forgiven for recoiling in horror at the sheer opaqueness of the technical jargon that is often used to frame it. So before we get into what a cryptocurrency is and how blockchain technology might change the world, let's discuss what blockchain actually is.

In the simplest terms, blockchain is a digital ledger of transactions, similar to the ledgers we have been using for hundreds of years to record sales and purchases. The function of this digital ledger is, in fact, pretty much identical to a traditional ledger in that it records debits and credits between two parties. The difference is who holds the ledger and who verifies the transactions.

With traditional transactions, a payment from one person to another involves some kind of intermediary to facilitate the transaction. Let's say Rob wants to transfer $20 to Melanie. He can either give her cash in the form of a $20 note, or he can use some kind of banking app to transfer the money directly to her bank account. In both cases, the bank serves as an intermediary and verifies the transaction whether Rob takes the money out of a cash machine or by an app when he makes a digital transfer. Ultimately, the bank decides if the transaction should proceed. The bank also holds a record of all the transactions made by Rob and is solely responsible for updating it whenever Rob debits or credits his account. In other words, the bank holds and controls the ledger, and everything goes through the bank.

That's a lot of responsibility given to the bank, so it's important that Rob feels he can trust his bank, otherwise he would not risk his money with them. He needs to feel confident that the bank will not defraud him, will not lose his money, will not be robbed, and will not disappear overnight.

This need for trust has underpinned pretty much every major behaviour and facet of the monolithic finance industry to the extent that, even when it was discovered that banks were being irresponsible with our money during the financial crisis of 2008, the government (another intermediary) chose to bail them out rather than risk destroying the final fragments of trust by letting them collapse.

Blockchains operate differently in one key respect: they are entirely decentralized. There is no central clearing house like a bank, and there is no central ledger held by one entity. Instead, the ledger is distributed across a vast network of computers, called nodes, each of which holds a copy of the entire ledger on their respective hard drives. These nodes are connected to one another via a piece of software called a peer-to-peer (P2P) client, which synchronizes data across the network of nodes and makes sure that everybody has the same version of the ledger at any given point in time.

When a new transaction is entered into a blockchain, it is first encrypted using state-of-the-art cryptographic technology. Once encrypted, the transaction is converted to something called a block, which is the term used for an encrypted group of new transactions. That block is then sent (or broadcasted) into the network of computer nodes where, once verified, it is passed on through the network and is added to the end of the ledger on everybody's computer, under the list of all previous blocks. This is called the chain, hence the tech is referred to as a blockchain.

Once approved and recorded into the ledger, the transaction can be completed. This is how cryptocurrencies like Bitcoin work.

CHAPTER 1

APPLICATIONS OF BLOCKCHAIN

Where things get really interesting is the applications of blockchain beyond cryptocurrencies like Bitcoin. Given that one of the underlying principles of the blockchain system is the secure, independent verification of a transaction, it's easy to imagine other ways in which this type of process can be valuable. Unsurprisingly, many such applications are already in use or are in development. Some of the best ones are:

1.	Smart contracts (Ethereum): Probably the most exciting blockchain development after Bitcoin. Smart contracts are blocks that contain code that must be executed in order for the contract to be fulfilled. The code can be anything, as long as a computer can execute it, but in simple terms, it means that you can use blockchain technology (with its independent verification, trustless architecture and security) to create a kind of escrow system for any kind of transaction. For example, if you're a web designer, you could create a contract that verifies if a new client's website is launched or not, and then automatically release the funds to you once it is. No more chasing or invoicing. Smart contracts are also being used to prove ownership of an asset, such as property or art. The potential for reducing fraud with this approach is enormous.

2.   Cloud storage (Storj): Cloud computing has revolutionized the web and brought about the advent of Big Data which has in turn, kick-started the new AI revolution. But most cloud-based systems are run on servers stored in single-location server farms, owned by a single entity (Amazon, Rackspace, Google etc).

This presents all the same problems as the banking system where your data is controlled by a single, opaque organization, which represents a single point of failure. Distributing data on a blockchain removes the trust issue entirely and also promises to increase reliability as it is so much harder to take a blockchain network down.

3.   Digital identification (ShoCard): Two of the biggest issues of our time are identity theft and data protection.

With vast centralized services such as Facebook holding so much data about us, and efforts by various developed-world governments to store digital information about their citizens in a central database, the potential for abuse of our personal data is terrifying. Blockchain technology offers a potential solution to this by wrapping your key data up into an encrypted block that can be verified by the blockchain network whenever you need to prove your identity. The applications of this range from the replacement of passports and I.D. cards to other areas such as replacing passwords. It could be huge.

4.   Digital voting: Highly topical in the wake of the investigation into Russia's influence on the recent U.S. presidential election, digital voting has long been suspected of being both unreliable and highly vulnerable to tampering.

Blockchain technology offers a way of verifying that a voter's vote was successfully sent while retaining their anonymity. It promises not only to reduce fraud in elections, but also to increase general voter turnout as people will be able to vote on their mobile devices.

Blockchain technology is still very much in its infancy and most of the applications are a long way from general use. Even Bitcoin, the most established blockchain platform, is subject to huge volatility, indicative of its relative newcomer status. However, the potential for blockchain to solve some of the major problems we face today makes it an extraordinarily, exciting and seductive technology to follow.

CHAPTER 2

BLOCKCHAIN TECHNOLOGY

These days, technology is scaling newer heights of success at an unbelievably fast pace. One of the latest triumphs in this direction is the evolution of the blockchain technology. This new technology has greatly influenced the finance sector. In fact, it was initially developed for bitcoins - the digital currency. But now, its application is found in a number of other things as well. So what is blockchain?

A DISTRIBUTED DATABASE

Imagine an electronic spreadsheet, which is copied an umpteenth number of times across a computer network. Now, imagine a computer network that can regularly update the spreadsheet on its own. This is a broad overview of blockchain. Blockchain holds information as a shared database. Moreover, this database gets reconciled continuously.

This approach has its own benefits. It does not allow the database to be stored at any single location. The records in it possess genuine public attribute and can be verified very easily. As there's no centralized version of the records, unauthorized users have no means to manipulate or corrupt the data. The blockchain distributed database is simultaneously hosted by millions of computers, making the data easily accessible to almost anyone across the virtual web.

To make the concept and the technology clearer, it is a good idea to discuss the Google Docs analogy.

GOOGLE DOCS ANALOGY FOR BLOCKCHAIN

After the advent of the eMail, the conventional way of sharing documents is to send a Microsoft Word document as an attachment to a recipient or recipients.

The recipients will take their sweet time to go through it before they send back the revised copy. In this approach, one needs to wait until receiving the return copy to see the changes made to the document.

This happens because the sender is locked out from making corrections until the recipient is done with the editing, and sends the document back. Contemporary databases do not allow two owners access to the same record at the same time. This is how banks maintain balances with their clients and account-holders.

In contrast to the set practice, Google Docs allow both parties to access the same document at the same time. Moreover, it also allows viewing a single version of the document to both of them simultaneously. Just like a shared ledger, Google Docs also acts as a shared document. The distributed part only becomes relevant when the sharing involves multiple users.

Blockchain technology is, in a way, an extension of this concept. However, it is important to point out here that the blockchain is not meant to share documents. Rather, it is just an analogy, which will help to have a clear-cut idea about this cutting-edge technology.

SALIENT BLOCKCHAIN FEATURES

Blockchain stores blocks of information across the network, that are identical. By virtue of this feature:

- The data or information cannot be controlled by any single, particular entity.

- There can't be any single failure point either.

- The data is held in a public network, which ensures absolute transparency in the overall procedure.

- The data stored in it cannot be corrupted.

DEMAND FOR BLOCKCHAIN DEVELOPERS

As stated earlier, blockchain technology has a very high application in the world of finance and banking. According to the World Bank, more than $430 billion USD in transfers were sent through it in 2015 alone. Thus, blockchain developers have significant demand in the market. Blockchain eliminates the payoff of the middlemen in such monetary transactions.

It was the invention of the GUI (Graphical User Interface), which facilitated the common man to access computers in the form of desktops. Similarly, the wallet application is the most common GUI used for blockchain technology. Users make use of the wallet to buy things they want using bitcoins or any other cryptocurrency.

With all this introduction, we can finally address, what is blockchain?

Blockchain is an irrefutably resourceful invention, which is practically bringing about a revolution in the global business market. Its evolution has brought with it a greater good, not only for businesses, but for its beneficiaries as well. Upon its revelation to the world, a vision of its operational activities is still unclear and so the question remains, what will blockchain become?

To continue, blockchain technology serves as a platform that allows the transit of digital information without the risk of being copied. It has, in a way, laid the foundation of a strong backbone of a new kind of internet space. Originally designed to deal with Bitcoin - trying to explain the layman about the functions of its algorithms, the hash functions, and digital signature property. Today, the technology buffs are finding other potential uses of this immaculate invention, which could pave the way to the onset of an entirely new business dealing process in the world.

Blockchain is a kind of algorithm and data distribution structure for the management of electronic cash without the intervention of any centralized administration. It is programmed to record all the financial transactions as well as everything that holds value.

CHAPTER 3

THE WORKING OF BLOCKCHAIN

Blockchain can be comprehended as Distributed Ledger technology, which was originally devised to support the bitcoin cryptocurrency. But post heavy criticism and rejection, the technology was revised for use in things more productive.

To give a clear picture, imagine a spreadsheet that's practically augmented many times across a plethora of computing systems. And then imagine that these networks are designed to update this spreadsheet from time to time. This is exactly what blockchain is.

Information that's stored on a blockchain is a shared sheet whose data is reconciled from time to time. It's a practical way that speaks to many obvious benefits. To begin with, the blockchain data doesn't exist in one single place. This means that everything stored in there is open for public view and verification. Further, there isn't any centralized information storing platform, which hackers can corrupt. It's practically accessed with over a million computing systems side-by-side, and its data can be consulted by any individual with an internet connection.

DURABILITY AND AUTHENTICITY OF BLOCKCHAIN

Blockchain technology is something that minims the internet space. It's chic robust in nature. Similar to offering data to the general public through the World Wide Web, blocks of authentic information are stored onto a blockchain platform which is identically visible on all networks.

Vital to note, blockchain cannot be controlled by a single person, entity or identity, and has no one point of failure as discussed earlier. Just like the internet has proven itself as a durable space since the last 30 years, blockchain too, will serve as an authentic, reliable global stage for business transactions as it continues to develop.

TRANSPARENCY AND INCORRUPTIBLE NATURE

Veterans of the industry claim that blockchain lives in a state of consciousness. It practically checks on itself every now and then. It's similar to a self-auditing technology where its network reconciles every transaction, known as a block, which happens at regular intervals.

This gives birth to two major properties of blockchain - it's highly transparent, and at the same time, it cannot be corrupted. Each and every transaction that takes place on this server is embedded within the network and is made visible to the public. Furthermore, to edit or omit information on blockchain asks for a humongous amount of effort and a strong computing power. Amid this, frauds can be easily identified. Hence, it's termed "incorruptible."

ACCOUNTABILITY AND THE REMOVAL OF TRUST

What are the advantages of this system over a banking or central clearing system? Why would Rob use Bitcoin instead of a normal currency?

The answer is trust. As mentioned before, with the banking system it is critical that Rob trusts his bank to protect his money and to handle it properly. To ensure that this happens, enormous regulatory systems exist to verify the actions of the banks and ensure they are fit for purpose.

Governments then regulate the regulators, creating a sort of tiered system of checks whose sole purpose is to help prevent mistakes and bad behavior. In other words, organizations like the Financial Services Authority exist precisely because banks can't be trusted on their own. And banks frequently make mistakes and misbehave, as we have seen too many times.

When you have a single source of authority, power tends to get abused or misused. The trust relationship between people and banks is awkward and precarious: we don't really trust them, but we don't feel there is much alternative.

Blockchain systems, on the other hand, don't need you to trust them at all. All transactions (or blocks) in a blockchain are verified by the nodes in the network before being added to the ledger, which means there is no single point of failure and no single approval channel. If a hacker wanted to successfully tamper with the ledger on a blockchain, they would have to simultaneously hack millions of computers, which is almost impossible. A hacker would also be arguably unable to bring a blockchain network down, as, again, they would need to be able to shut down every single computer in a network of computers distributed around the world.

The encryption process itself is also a key factor. Blockchains, like Bitcoin, use deliberately difficult processes for their verification procedure. In the case of Bitcoin, blocks are verified by nodes performing a deliberate processor- and time-intensive series of calculations, often in the form of puzzles or complex mathematical problems, which mean that verification is neither instant nor accessible. Nodes that do commit the resource to verification of blocks are rewarded with a transaction fee and a bounty of newly-minted Bitcoins. This has the function of both incentivizing people to become nodes (because processing blocks like this require pretty powerful computers and a lot of electricity), whilst also handling the process of generating - or minting - units of the currency. This is referred to as mining because it involves a considerable amount of effort (by a computer, in this case) to produce a new commodity. It also means that transactions are verified by the most independent way possible, more independent than a government-regulated organization like the FSA.

This decentralized, democratic and highly secure nature of blockchains means that they can function without the need for regulation (they are self-regulating), government or another opaque intermediary. They work because people don't trust each other, rather than in spite of. Let the significance of that sink in for a while and the excitement around blockchain starts to make sense.

CHAPTER 4

USERS OF BLOCKCHAIN

There isn't a defined rule or regulation about who shall or can make use of this immaculate technology. Though at present, its potential users are banks, commercial giants, and global economies only, but the technology is open for the day to day transactions of the general public as well. The only drawback blockchain is facing is global acceptance. Dozens of large financial institutions, including many of the world's major banks, have already launched initiatives to explore blockchain's potential.

As applied in the Bitcoin context, blockchain is a decentralized, public ledger that contains the details of every Bitcoin transaction that has ever been completed. Due to a number of innovative technical protocols, the ledger has proven to be exceptionally accurate and secure.

Interest in the technology exploded when it became clear that blockchain can be used to document the transfer of any digital asset, record the ownership of physical and intellectual property, and establish rights through smart contracts, among other applications. By reordering and automating complex, labor-intensive processes, the technology can enable organizations to operate both faster and more cheaply.

Financial institutions are exploring a variety of opportunities to use blockchain, including applications to improve and enhance currency exchange, supply chain management, trade execution and settlement, remittance, peer-to-peer transfers, micropayments, asset registration, correspondent banking and regulatory reporting.

Highlighting the potential for banks, Santander issued a report in 2015 estimating that blockchain "could reduce banks' infrastructure costs attributable to cross-border payments, securities trading and regulatory compliance by between US$15 – 20 billion per annum by 2022." And there is a reason to believe the actual figure may be higher.

For most large financial institutions that are exploring blockchain opportunities, 2018 will be a year of continued innovation and experimentation. But these activities are only a prelude to profound changes throughout the financial sector.

Blockchain is a technology that was initially developed for Bitcoin, the cryptocurrency. It is a distributed ledger or database that is operated by a peer-to-peer network of unaffiliated participants. Using computers running sophisticated algorithms, these participants, so-called Bitcoin "miners", process transactions according to strict protocols that ensure a very high degree of accuracy and security.

Anyone can participate—the blockchain is fully transparent and available to all—but only the miners that are the first to process an individual transaction are compensated.

As individual transactions are processed and verified by other miners on the network, they are bundled into groups called blocks; blocks of transactions are linked together to make the blockchain. Every Bitcoin transaction is permanently recorded in the Bitcoin blockchain for all to see, creating an ever-growing historic record of activity. The mining process creates continuous, decentralized monitoring by every computer on the network and ensures the accuracy and security of the blockchain record.

Blockchain technology revolutionizes the transaction process by dispersing control and providing total transparency, obviating the need for the type of middlemen or centralized authorities that traditionally conduct, authorize or verify transactions.

The use of blockchain is not limited to Bitcoin or other cryptocurrencies. Blockchain has the potential to transform how business and government work in a wide variety of contexts. Blockchain can be used to record and track the details of any transaction or ownership of any asset, including tangible assets such as real estate and intangible assets such as intellectual property. It can also be used to automate contracts, dramatically simplifying the process of creating and executing them.

The perception of blockchain's potential is reflected in investment trends. According to Goldman Sachs, venture capital (VC) firms invested almost a billion dollars in the technology over the last three years, with about half of that amount invested in 2015 As we will see, financial institutions are among the biggest investors in blockchain, reflecting a growing belief that the technology may actually have its greatest impact in the financial services sector.

CHAPTER 5

WHAT IS BITCOIN?

Bitcoins have become a very well known and popular form of currency over time. Though, what exactly is Bitcoin? This chapter will go over the in's and out's of this currency that popped up out of nowhere and spread like a wildfire. What makes it different from normal currencies?

Bitcoin is a digital currency, it is not printed and never will be. They are held electronically and nobody has control over it either. They're produced by people and businesses, creating the first ever form of money known as a cryptocurrency. While normal currencies are seen in the real world, Bitcoin runs through billions of computers all around the world. From Bitcoin in the United States to Bitcoin in China, it has become a global currency. However, the biggest distinction it has from other currencies is that it is decentralized. This means that no specific company or bank owns it.

WHO CREATED BITCOIN?

The technology was created by an individual hiding under an identity named Satoshi Nakamoto. To this day, the creator/creators of the system never materialized, maintaining an anonymous status.

Bitcoins are not printed like traditional currencies as there are no physical representations for the cryptocurrency; it is produced by users and numerous businesses through a process called mining. This is where dedicated software solves mathematical problems in exchange for the virtual currency.

A user takes control of it using electronic devices, which also serves as a medium to complete transactions with the help of numerous platforms. It is also kept and secured with the employment of virtual wallets.

WHO PRINTS BITCOINS?

As mentioned earlier, the simple answer is nobody. Bitcoin is not a printed currency, it is a digital one. You can even conduct transactions online using bitcoins. So you can't churn out unlimited bitcoins? Absolutely not. Bitcoin is designed to never "mine" more than 21 million bitcoins into the world at one time. Although they can be broken up into smaller amounts. One hundred millionth of a bitcoin is called a "Satoshi", after its creator.

WHAT IS BITCOIN BASED ON?

For appearances mostly and conventional use, Bitcoin is based on gold and silver. However, the truth is that Bitcoin is actually based on pure mathematics. It has nothing to hide either as it's an open source. So anyone can look into it to see if it's running the way they claim.

HISTORY OF BITCOIN

Bitcoin is the premier cryptocurrency in the world. It is a peer-to-peer currency and transaction system based on a decentralized consensus-based public ledger called blockchain that records all transactions.

The bitcoin was envisaged in 2008 by Satoshi Nakamoto but it was a product of many decades of research into cryptography and blockchain and not just one guy's work. It was the utopian dream of cryptographers and free trade advocates to have a borderless, decentralized currency based on the blockchain. Their dream is now a reality with the growing popularity of bitcoin around the world.

Now, the cryptocurrency was first deployed over the consensus-based blockchain in 2009 and the same year it was traded for the very first time. In July 2010, the price of bitcoin was just 8 cents and the number of miners and nodes was quite less compared to tens of thousands in number right now.

Within the space of one year, the new alternative currency had risen to $1 and it was becoming an interesting prospect for the future.

Mining was relatively easy and people were making good money making trades and even paying with it in some cases.

Within six months, the currency had doubled again to $2. While the price of bitcoin is not stable at a particular price point, it has been showing this pattern of insane growth for some time. In July 2011 at one point, the coin went bonkers and the record-high $31 price point was achieved but the market soon realized that it was overvalued compared to the gains made on the ground and it recorrected it back to $2.

December 2012 saw a healthy increase to $13 but soon enough, the price was going to explode. Within four months until April 2013, the price had increased to a whopping $266. It corrected itself later on back to $100 but this astronomical increase in price rose it stardom for the very first time and people started debating about an actual real-world scenario with Bitcoin.

The more you read about it, the more it became clear that the currency was the future as it had no one to manipulate it or impose itself on it. Everything had to be done with complete consensus and that was what made it so strong and free.

So 2013 was the breakthrough year for the currency. Big companies began to publicly favor the acceptance of bitcoin and blockchain became a popular subject for Computer Science programs. Many people then thought that bitcoin had served its purpose and now it would settle down.

But, the currency became even more popular, with bitcoin ATMs being set up around the world and other competitors started flexing their muscles at different angles of the market. Ethereum developed the first programmable blockchain and Litecoin and

Ripple started themselves as cheaper and faster alternatives to bitcoin.

The magical figure of $1000 was first breached in January 2017 and since then it had increased four times already until September. It is truly a remarkable achievement for a coin that was only worth 8 cents just seven years back.

Bitcoin even survived a hard fork on August 1, 2017, and had risen nearly 70% since then while even the fork bitcoin cash has managed to post some success. All of it is due to the appeal of the coin and stellar blockchain technology behind it. Presently one Bitcoin is over $16,000.

While conventional economists argue that it is a bubble and the whole crypto world would collapse, it is just not so. There is no such bubble since it is an observable fact that it has, in fact, eaten away the shares of the fiat currencies and money transaction corporations. The future is extremely bright for many different cryptocurrencies in the blockchain space. While it won't rise forever, and will certainly go down before it goes up again, it is truly an interesting piece of programming.

CHAPTER 6

CHARACTERISTICS OF BITCOIN

Bitcoin has the characteristics of traditional currencies such as purchasing power and investment applications that use online trading instruments. It works just like conventional money, except that it can only exist in the digital world.

One of its unique attributes that cannot be matched by fiat currency is that it is decentralized. This digital currency does not run under a governing body or an institution, which means it cannot be controlled by these entities and gives users full ownership of their bitcoins.

Moreover, bitcoin transactions occur with the use of bitcoin addresses, which are not linked to names, addresses, or personal information asked for by traditional payment systems. In order to make a transaction, the owner must know the corresponding private key to the bitcoin address and must digitally sign the transaction. Every single bitcoin transaction is stored in a ledger that anyone can access, and this is called a blockchain. Each bitcoin is registered to a bitcoin address. If a user has a publicly used address, its information is shared for everyone to see, without its user's information of course.

Accounts are easy to create, unlike conventional banks that requests for countless information, which may put its users in jeopardy due to the frauds and schemes surrounding the system.

Furthermore, bitcoin transaction fees will always be small in number. Apart from near-instant completion of processing, no fees are known to be significant enough to put a dent in one's account.

HOW DOES BITCOIN WORK?

The finer details of how Bitcoin works can be tricky to understand because it is not under central control like conventional currency. Instead, every transaction is collectively approved by a network of users. There are no coins and no notes, no bullion held in a vault, but the Bitcoin supply is finite and it will stop at 21 million.

Every 10 minutes, 25 bitcoins are found by Bitcoin "miners", and every 4 years the number of bitcoins released will halve until the limit is reached. This means that there will be no further release of bitcoins after 2140.

CONCLUSION

With no accountability to anyone, bitcoins are fairly unique. Bitcoins are sovereign with their distinct rules, and aren't printed in a clandestine manner by any bank, but mined. They're produced digitally by a good number of people involved in a colossal network or community. Miners usually employ enormous computing power, and a great deal of competition is involved in bitcoin mining. Computers work to solve complex mathematical problems. The competing miners earn bitcoins in the process by solving these problems.

However, the complexity of these problems intensifies day by day. Transactions via the bitcoin network are relentless and incessant, and keeping track of these transactions is fairly systematic. The bitcoin network is methodical and during a given time span, all transactions are collected in a block. Miners are supposed to validate transactions and everything is listed in a general ledger, which is simply a collection of blocks termed blockchain. The blockchain actually holds the key to the details of any transaction made across various bitcoin addresses.